Luscious Glass Cage

Jessica Raschke

Luscious Glass Cage

For all the elsewhere

Luscious Glass Cage
ISBN 978 1 74027 501 9
Copyright © text Jessica Raschke 2008
Copyright © cover art and design Allison Colpoys 2008

First published 2008
Reprinted 2016

Ginninderra Press
PO Box 3461 Port Adelaide SA 5015
www.ginninderrapress.com.au

Contents

glass cage	7
moon persuasion	8
taken hunch	9
puzzle tracings	10
sink you	11
nervy words	12
lonely tongue	13
skinbox shame	14
undiscovered looming	15
bristle crunch	16
the glory promise	17
please gain	19
duplicated tracings	20
the once should	21
strung-up organ	23
natural huskiness	25
platitudes and lace	26
applause	27
changing of the bones	28
glacial trimmings	30
drama sections	31
self-amplify	32
angst swallow	33
the fingertip blur	34
meltings	35
raised lovers	36
quiver grinding	37
insides my out	38
un-unique entry	39
break the glass cage	40
general universe	41

glass cage

this sparkling glass cage
shelters tetchy sorts of views

moon persuasion

for some gentle persuasion
try the cloak of the moon
collapse in its burn
mourn in its horizons
collude in its cloak
grave gracious booming
bursting punctuated blind
wear the moon in a moment

(and build it up)
(yes, build it)
(that bursting ounce of moon conviction)
(and cloak it up)
(yes, cloak it)
(you, the gently persuaded)

taken hunch

take a hunch
and take it over
strike a fist across its blade
punch its firmness
pound its sharpness

do it

until

it is

hunched over

take a hunch
and take it in
swallow it in the hand
knuckle it up with tensions
and let it bleed into its whiteness

see that hunch
it's taken over
it's gripped
and taken over
see that hunch
where it sits
in that porous rock-form hand

puzzle tracings

your tracings
they are fondled
by those modern eyelids
they are shut
and overshadowed
by shapeless puzzle forms
those tracings
they are laid out
like a deceptive valiant ruse

and here I am
fingering the puzzle
and here I am
with the puzzle
neither solving
nor picking up
its little jagged little bits

and here I am
another puzzle
(being quietly constructed)
and here I am
another puzzle
(being felt up)
and here I am
just a puzzle
(in your luscious pervy gaze)

sink you

there goes you
a package of wisdom
a steaming sultry brew

there goes you
a history a story
with bits for me
(and not you)

there goes some sinking
some glorious kind of view

there is just one question
can I sink you deeper through

there is reluctance in your story
you wish to halt it some

but permit me to caress this story
and let me sink you deeper through

nervy words

why hesitate a word
why fashion it furthermore
why stroke an arm for comfort
why not burst all of you through

in the air
hangs the world
it throbs with muscle and strength
in the air
there is ease
a tender home
for nervy words
all of this is easy
just burst
some more
of you
through

lonely tongue

the fork in your tongue grows crooked
it is random, bent and cruel
it hinges on some anger
like it might be lonely too

skinbox shame

the shame comes in a package
in this tall and handsome type
but the skinbox, it bellows
with piercing lashes of foreign breath
and the skinbox, it grips
with knuckles over-bent
but the skinbox, it attempts
to hold its cacophonous breath

think it through!
it thinks it through!
attempts to bite it
all the way through
watch it!
watch out!

hurts/
crashes/
splashes/
burns/

(knuckles are contracted)
(thoughts are now fractured)

but the itching skinbox
it shimmers
but the itching skinbox
it smiles

undiscovered looming

detect the presence of the looming
the gentle presence of the union
you're a lover
you're a lover
undiscovered
lover

bristle crunch

crunch those bristles around my open mouth

(you know it)
(don't you)

not all invitations are this honest

such guardedness/
it bristles/
it collapses/
and/
it does so/
with wet wanting/

crunch those bristles around my open mouth

the glory promise

unsolve this puzzle
yes, bitch the pieces up
trundle and rumble and
yes, bitch them up
like a potent forgotten history
crammed with your lost wanting

this is what it looks like:

snappy pot-shots
snappy smarts
snappy smiles

here comes pleasure:

in a breathy moment
in the flash of a sunray
in a flutter of some starshine
in the treasure of a heart

in a moment
there was pleasure

(yes)

in a moment
there was pleasure

and then
a gloomy silence follows
here comes
a burst of forgotten wanting

you always felt promised
like unpaid glory
was owed
to you

please gain

please admire this containment
for it took so long
to fashion
take note of the subtle inflections
in this twisty husky voice

please gain some satisfaction
soaked in glorious easiness
please admire this containment

oh please
just please
please do

this exterior is my monument
a space for veneration
this exterior is only worthy
once it receives celebration

oh please
just please
send me
polite
performed
applause

duplicated tracings

what kinds of records are duplicated
your tracings are public now
careless you, thoughtless you
why leave it all behind
so peculiarly
so demurely
so abruptly

the once should

let me, once
just allow me, once
dissolve memories of the propers
and the shoulds

let me say it, once
just hear me, once:

these coverings are protectors
transparent flimsy layers
they comfort for a flash
until again the chills set in

let me penetrate, once
just enter me, once
or, please, do tell me
what this convenient deception is for

it flickers through, once
and it is discarded, once

it reveals
it all
all of life's
little lies

it confirms
it all
all of life's
evidence

let me/
once
just allow me/
once

strung-up organ

damn me for my passions
condemn me for my heart
on the line it goes
again

for the wind/
for the picking/
for the faking/

it has eyes and lips
with which to see and talk

damn me again
for that strung-up heart

it flickers/
it twitches/
it begs/

it likes the look of *you*
it likes the sound of *you*

damn that strung-up organ
standing in as me
a frisky winded decoy
a punctured faked-up soul
place that organ in both your hands

and

Crunch/
it
Spit/
it
Damn/
it

natural huskiness

there she goes,
prohibited!
he asks she is,
uninhibited!
he croons in the sultry darkness
glides wings
graciously
clumsily
seductively
and with an expansive shining heart

(the mastery is no guise)

oh yes!

his presence shimmers
and
his footsteps are of nature
and
they step in the way of truth

huskiness not from husk
depths without deepness

(what I'm saying is)

he is easy

he is something

uninhibited

platitudes and lace

what can happen
while I wear such luscious lace
and dressed it as my face

(oh yes, the platitudes will escalate!)
(oh yes, love will flow in wet explosions!)
(oh yes, yes, love will flood this little ravine of mine!)

applause

listen to them
those thunderous claps
to those crunching slaps

generous serves of elemental furies
rumbling as bloodied juries

listen to them
those fouled-up adjudicators
screaming in choral applause

listen to them
those thunderous claps
throwing roars among the mutes

changing of the bones

there are bones breaking in resistance
urging for reparation through a declaration

my mind has changed
my judgements have wronged us
my fear has crippled our hearts

and now
my bravado

it has peaked

and now
it will happen

I will drop one life
forsake it

I will take the other
embrace it

this one, we know
this one, our melting souls

from the deep shallows
I will build it

(a life-union)

I will allow for a peak
I will allow it to keep reaching

to live
breathing
to live
infinitely
to live
as it will
like
soulful
assurance

this is what stops bones from breaking
the only way to soothe certain aching

glacial trimmings

your trimmings are glaciers
with hunky tips that glisten
they blind with their melting
they are staving off their freedom
…away from the sun

the edgeless sections shift
into crumpled waters below
these glacial trimmings
frame the fantasy
they shift it
they shift
these are your glacial trimmings
…burdened by a sun

drama sections

in the broken sections of the drama
lie some jealous little shards
they move themselves as troopers
into veins and dotted red cells
they possess small histories
that are laid down for the shattering
and those broken sections:

they forget their wholes
they relish in their self-destruction

(it was once called self-murder)

pinioned/
staked/
hanged/
paraded/

not shame not brokenness
only the surfacing of some deepness
a damned public viewing
of a circle of the broken
they are sections
that are inlaid
they are
set in fleshy faces
they are
suddenly relieved
in the broken sections of the drama

self-amplify

amplify the resonance
amplify your *self*
open an ear
spiral it down
and broaden the funnel
(let the pleasure flow)
because
it's all
your
self

angst swallow

swallow the angst and love it
savour its enervating lotion
for it is smooth
for it is drippy

swallow the fucking and love it
fall and thrall and let me break
for what is it
just tough relieving
my little fuckable bitten delight

the fingertip blur

place them/
those handfuls of questing fingers
place them/
into bumps unfelt and undetected
place them/
and blur fingertip perceptions
place them/
and unshine them with unpassion
place them/
away from all my surfaces
place them/
cradle them deepest in me
place them/
where we please
and place them/
once more
and again

meltings

dropped dreams left to melt
spread now in their wetness and neglect
a layering of invisible remains
only known now by knowing eyes
do you recall where you left them
they are there
knocking up from the earth
you are slipping among their will
you are sliding in their melting
you are splashed
you are spoiled
in all of those
disguised
wet dreamings

raised lovers

the raise of an eyebrow
a confession to her, the 'oh my lover'
this wilfulness is exhausted
as he embraces her, the not 'oh my lover'
his arms collapse away among imagined sighs
breathe again
breathe
tremble in the ripples
collapse again
fold into yourself
with 'oh my lover'
just one more time
and then
just one more time
again
let 'oh my lover' forget the moment
desires explode into energies
every thing rumbles
every little thing
what a fucking memory
what a fucking sigh
where are you now
'oh my lover'
detected
revealed
shamed (in the) breaths of a lie

quiver grinding

will the quiver, will the bones
will the shame, will the grinding
expose the innards of this artless little heart
stuck, stuck, stuck

something in your promises
gave the heartbeats puff
they huffed, almost pounding
fed by the coy
the oh so coy
the careful not to hurt

but your wave of flimsy gestures
washed away the sweetness
stretched it out
a spread of veins
now set in dusty blood

place an eye to those innards
see the scratchings in the lining
the rehearsed delicacy was aimless
it swept afflictions all the way

insides my out

no, my insides are not my out
and this darkness is not a void
perhaps it's something else
a vague kind of joke
something half-hearted
something not buried
like meaning
this is as heavy as it is light
and your gravity its only weight
be blind, be bright, be pleased
but my insides are not my out

un-unique entry

There is another hint of it in the loins.
An un-unique and repetitive sensation.
The urge to become an entry point.
The entry point.

break the glass cage

watch that painful precious thing
that compels a shattering of the guard
happening over an image
of falling into myself
guided by you
held by you
drape me in your heartbeats
brush your breath against mine
place my hand over your heart
graciously, easily
the tender initiation into the next space
a gentle shift into shared dreams

general universe

this little universe I construct
is no universe at all
it's a thinning layer of layer
a general kind of polish

really

it's just a little hint of deepness
it just suggests a universe
no more than a layer of layer
just a general kind of place

www.ingramcontent.com/pod-product-compliance
Lightning Source LLC
Chambersburg PA
CBHW062207100526
44589CB00014B/1989